Storytime
with the Millers

Mildred A. Martin

Illustrated by **Anthony Baker**

Miller Family Series

Green Pastures Press

Scripture Verses are taken from
the King James Version

Storytime with the Millers

Copyright 1992, 1994 by Mildred A. Martin

Green Pastures Press
HC 67, Box 91-A, Mifflin, PA 17058

Children's Stories

Miller Family Series

Printed in the United States of America

ISBN   1-884377-00-9   Paperback

Table of Contents

Therefore if thine enemy hunger, feed him.
Romans 12:20.

The Indians and the Cookies

It was a sunny Sunday afternoon in spring, and the three Martin boys were having a wonderful time playing Indians. Amos, the oldest, was the chief; he had a paper headband adorned with feathers. Joel had Daddy's small hatchet for a tomahawk to cut up wood for the campfire. Micah, with one feather stuck into his blond thatch of hair, was gathering food for the tribe: handfuls of tasty mint leaves from the tea patch, and bark chips for pemmican.

The three boys often played Indians,

but today they had discovered their best campsite yet! Over at the edge of the Martin's yard, there was a large bush with a funny name: Bridal Wreath. Under its leafy branches was the perfect spot for a hideout . . . cool, green, and private. Amos and Joel brought several handfuls of old shingles from the garage, and used them to build a wall up to the bottom branches of the bush.

"Now, nobody can see into our camp, if they go past on the road!" Amos told his brothers happily.

"You know what?" said Joel, crawling from the hide-out again to examine the outside. "This wall of shingles makes our hut look just like a real bark wigwam. An

Iroquois wigwam!"

"Who were the Iroquois?" wondered 5-year-old Micah.

"They were the Indians who lived here in Ohio in the old days. We learned about them in school," Joel replied.

Suddenly the three Indians heard voices. Across the road and up a steep bank of dirt, their eyes followed the sound. There in the neighbor's garden were two teenage boys. They were hard at work under the hot sun, pulling weeds and picking up rocks! "Aren't you glad *we* don't believe in working on Sunday?" Amos asked his brothers in a low voice. Giggling, the boys plunged back into the shelter of their wigwam.

But it was too late: the neighbor boys had spotted the Martins too. "What are you little guys doing?" came a rough shout from the hillside garden. Plop! . . . A large clod of earth hurtled across the road and struck Amos's shingle wall. Roaring with laughter, the boys tossed another volley of dirt clumps and rocks at the tempting target.

"Hey!" cried Amos, poking his head out of the damaged wigwam. "You stop that, Jason! You almost hit Micah with a rock." But his only answer was a mocking laugh as another dirt clod whistled past, dangerously close to Amos' head.

Hastily grabbing a few possessions, the three Indians scrambled out of their threatened wigwam and sadly retreated to the middle of the yard. Sitting Indian-style on the grass, they held a council. "Those boys are an enemy tribe, and they're shooting missiles at us!" declared Micah.

"Indians don't have missiles, silly," returned Joel.

"We don't want to be *fighting* Indians," Amos said thoughtfully. "How can we make peace with them?" He jumped to his feet. "I know how!" he called, dashing for the house.

"Mom!" Amos exclaimed as he burst into the kitchen. "May I have some cookies to take up to Jason and Matt? Then maybe they will leave us in peace!"

Mama had been observing her sons' problem from the kitchen window. "Why, I think that would be a good idea, Amos!" she answered approvingly. Going to the cupboard she took out some special cookies: big, soft, homemade cookies with gaily colored sprinkles of candy on top. "Be sure you speak politely and nicely," she admonished as she folded the cookies into two white paper napkins.

Joel and Micah watched anxiously as Amos trotted uphill with his offering. "Hey, Jason!" he called in a friendly tone. The big boys looked at him suspiciously, but laid down their hoes and came over. "You boys have been working so hard throwing dirt at us, I thought you might

be hungry! Here are some cookies," Amos said kindly.

"I bet you've got stones, not cookies," Matt growled.

"No, it's cookies for you! Here," Amos held out the treat.

"Oh! well, uh, thanks, I guess," stammered the surprised boys. They returned to their work with their mouths full of cookies, as Amos skipped triumphantly back down the hill.

Soon the Martin tribe of Indians moved into their wigwam once more. This time they were safe, since they had made enemies into friends . . . and this time they had some cookies to eat, too!

Children, obey your parents in the Lord, for this is right. Ephesians 6:1.

Paul in the Pit

When Paul was three years old, his family moved onto a dairy farm. Paul was excited. There were so many things to see! Best of all was the big barn, with its rows of stalls, interesting tools, and wagons. There were piles of hay bales and all kinds of big machines.

Paul's dad bought a lot of cows, and some little calves, too. Paul was a bit scared of those big cows! His parents told him he must not get too close to them, because some cows will kick little boys.

Paul had four older brothers, and they helped Dad with the chores in the barn. Sometimes Paul helped, too, when they were feeding the calves. At other times Mom wanted him to stay in the house. Then Paul was sad. He wished he would be big enough to milk cows, too.

One afternoon when Paul awoke from his nap he heard the rattle of milk cans and the mooing of cows from the barn. "Mom, may I go to the barn today?" he asked.

"No, Paul," said Mom. "You'd better stay with me. You may go out with me later when I wash the milk buckets."

Paul got out his toy animals and started to make a farm of his own on the floor. He set up four little fences to make a pen for his cows, and pretended to feed them hay. He had a toy horse, too, and made it gallop around the farm.

Soon Paul got tired of playing farm. He wanted to go out to the *real* farm, and see *real* animals.

Mom went upstairs with her arms full of clothes she had washed that day. Paul wandered over to the window and looked out. He could see the barn. He wanted to go out there so much. Then he had an idea! Surely Mom would not care if he went out and stood in the driveway so he could see the barn better.

Paul looked around. Mom was still upstairs. He put on his boots, then quietly opened the door and went outside. He felt guilty all the time, because he knew he was doing something Mom had said he must not do.

When Paul reached the driveway, he stood there for only a moment. He looked back toward the house. Mom did not call and tell him to come back, so he went on. Soon he had slipped through the door into the milkhouse at the end of the barn.

Paul played in the milkhouse for a minute, then he quietly went on into the main part of the barn. Paul knew he was disobeying, so he did not stop to talk to Dad and the boys. They did not see that he was in the barn. He stood in the corner and watched as they milked the big cows.

Paul knew where he wanted to go - - to the calf pens. He stood by the pens and watched the little calves for awhile. Then he wanted something else to do.

At the end of the barn was a big manure pit. Paul went there next. He stood on the edge of the pit and wrinkled his nose. "Phew!" he thought. "That manure does not smell good."

Paul found a stick and poked it into the manure. That was fun, so he poked in the manure some more.

Suddenly Paul's foot slipped and he had to take a quick step forward to keep his balance. PLOP! Down went Paul's one foot into the manure. PLOP! Down went the other foot, too.

Paul was so scared he didn't know what to do. The sticky manure was already higher than his knees, and he was sinking deeper all the time. How he wished he had obeyed Mom and stayed in the house. He struggled and tried to walk out of the pit, but that just made him sink deeper.

At last Paul found his voice. "DADDY!" he called. "DAA-DEE! DAAA-DEEEE!"

Paul's big brother, Thomas, was working near the end of the barn. He thought he heard something. Was Paul crying? "No, it is not Paul," he thought. "Paul is in the house with Mom."

"DAAAA-DEEEE!"

Thomas heard the sound again. He set his bucket down and went in the direction

of the sound. When he came to the manure pit, his eyes bulged with shock. There, on top of the manure pit was someone's head. It was his little brother's head. Paul had sunk all the way to his neck, and could no longer scream, but he rolled his frightened eyes at Thomas.

Thomas turned and ran back into the barn. He was crying, too. "Daddy, come quick. Oh, please, come quick!" Then he ran back to the pit.

Dad dropped what he had been doing and came running. He knew something terrible must have happened. When he saw Paul in the pit, he moved even faster. It was not easy to pull him out of the manure, but at last Paul was standing on solid ground again. Oh, how very dirty he was!

Dad and Mom cleaned Paul, then Dad sat with Paul on his lap. He talked to him for a long time. Paul could not understand everything Dad said, but there were two things he understood very well. He had come close to drowning in the manure pit, and it was his disobedience that had caused all the trouble.

Paul would remember that day for the rest of his life — the day he learned how serious it can be to disobey.

Behold, to obey is better than sacrifice.
I Samuel 15:22.

The Best Way to Help

It was Friday afternoon, and six-year-old Sharon was all excited. They were having company for supper! Sharon loved to have company, especially when there would be children along. Tonight Preacher Alvin's family was coming, and their youngest daughter was near Sharon's age.

Mama was busy in the kitchen. "What are you making for supper?" Sharon asked.

"I'm making chicken, with dressing

22

and potatoes," answered Mama. "And I think I'll make cupcakes, too."

"Cupcakes!" squealed Sharon. She loved cupcakes, and Mama so seldom made them. "I'll peel the potatoes for you," she offered. "Remember, you showed me how last week."

Mama hesitated. "I guess I'll do the potatoes tonight. It will take a lot, and we don't have much time. But you may straighten up the living room. You can put all the toys away, and dust the tops of the furniture."

"Oh, Mom," Sharon grumbled. "I clean up the living room *every* day. I want to help you with supper."

"Sharon, the best way to help me is to

do what I tell you," Mama said. "I will let you help me in the kitchen later."

Sharon tidied up the living room. She tried to do a good job. She made sure all the toys were picked up, even those in the out-of-the-way places. She straightened the spread on the couch. She dusted the furniture, and set all the old *Family Life's* straight in the magazine rack. Then she came out into the kitchen.

"What shall I do next?" she asked.

"You may set the table," Mama said. "Set eleven places. Then you may put these cupcake papers into the pans."

Now that was work Sharon enjoyed! That was *really* helping to get ready for company. She set the table neatly. Then she took the package of cupcake papers and put them carefully into the pan, one by one.

Then Baby Laura let out a cry from the bedroom. She was waking from her nap. Mama brought her downstairs, fed her, and set her on the floor. But she still fussed. She wanted to be held. "Sharon, you will have to take care of her for me now," Mama said. "Please try bringing her a few toys. Play with her, and try hard to keep her happy."

"But Mom," Sharon wailed. "I want to help you!"

Mama laughed. "Sharon, if you take care of Baby Laura so I can get supper, that *is* helping me. If you don't keep her happy, then I can't work. Remember, the best way to help me is to do what you are told."

Sharon brought a few toys and played with the baby while Mama mixed the cupcake dough. She mixed flour and sugar and other things, and beat it a few minutes. "Now," Mama said. "That's all ready to put into the pans."

Just then Dad came to the door. "I'm sorry, but I need your help for just a few minutes," he said. "I want to move something, and the little boys aren't strong enough to help me."

"All right," Mama said. She hurried out with Dad.

Sharon plopped Laura on the floor.

She began to cry, but Sharon ignored her. This was her chance to really help Mama. She would put the cupcake dough into the pans! *I'll do it quickly, then she will see that I can!* Sharon thought.

Sharon was just barely tall enough to see into the mixing bowl on the counter top. Carefully she took the big spoon and dipped batter into the cupcake pan. She knew enough not to fill it all the way. When she thought she had enough batter in the first one, she went on to the next one. Some of the batter spilled, but she licked it up with her finger. Finally the first pan was filled! Sharon was pleased with herself.

Sharon stood on tiptoes to reach across the filled pan to get the empty one. Then it

happened! Her elbow pushed the edge of the full pan.

KER-PLUNK! The whole pan tipped, spilling all the cupcake batter. Down it went, splashing on the cupboard doors, on the floor, and all over Sharon.

Poor Sharon! She was so sorry. But it was too late. She knew she deserved to be punished. Instead of helping Mama, she had just made another big mess for Mama to clean up. And she had ruined all that good cupcake batter, too.

Mama's words flashed through Sharon's head. "The best way to help is to do what you are told." How she wished she had obeyed, and not tried to do something Mama had not told her to do.

Whatsoever thy hand findeth to do, do it with thy might. Ecclesiastes 9:10.

Boys and Toys

"Amos and Joel!" called Mama. "Come here. I have some work for you to do."

Amos and Joel were good workers. They knew that everyone had to do his share of the work. Usually they worked cheerfully and quickly. There were so many things they could do. Amos was five. He could weed in the garden, take care of the baby, and round up the goats when they got loose. He could fold the diapers, and sometimes he even went on carpenter jobs with Daddy.

Joel was three. He could set the table, run errands, and hand Mama the clothes pins when she hung up the wash. He could water the plants, too.

But there was one job Amos and Joel had to do twice a day, and they did not like to do it. They had to pick up all their toys before lunch and before bedtime. They got so tired of picking up toys. They did not work fast. They poked around. And the longer the job took, the more they hated it.

"Come and pick up your toys now," said Mama. "Then we will walk down to the neighbors and get eggs."

"Oh, goodie, goodie!" the boys cried. They loved to go to the neighbors. They

liked to play with the neighbors' children and their toys.

"You will have to hurry," Mama said. "I want to go as soon as I have given baby Micah his bath."

The boys were excited about going to the neighbors' house. They picked up toys for a few minutes. But there were so many more toys on the floor, and soon they slowed down. Amos began to tease Joel. Joel grabbed Amos' leg and they started tussling on the floor.

"Boys!" Daddy said. He was working at his desk. "You are not being obedient. Mama told you to pick up your toys."

Amos and Joel got busy. They picked up a few toys, but the job still looked so big. Soon they were playing again. They were playing with the toys instead of picking them up.

Mama called to Daddy. He went into the bedroom to talk to her. "I hate to go without them. They always like to go to the neighbors. But they did not obey," Mama said.

"Go ahead," Daddy said. "I will be here with them. This punishment might help more than a spanking."

Mama dressed the baby to take him outside. She picked up a bag for the eggs. "Good-bye, boys!" she said. "You poked around so long with your work that I have to go without you."

Amos and Joel jumped up and began

to cry. They tried to scoop up toys in big handfuls. But they were too late. Soon Mama was walking down the lane.

"I hope you will remember this, so it will not have to happen again," said Daddy. "Do your work right away, then you will be ready to go along next time."

Amos and Joel tried hard to remember. They did not want to be left behind again.

Timmy Is Responsible

"Dad, may I have a rabbit?" asked Timmy. "I want a rabbit of my own, to keep in that old hutch behind our shed."

This was not the first time Timmy had asked his parents to let him keep a rabbit. But they always said he was too young.

"A rabbit is a real live animal," Dad said now. "It would need to be fed and cared for every day. If you forgot, your rabbit would suffer."

"Aw, I wouldn't forget to take care of my rabbit," Timmy said. "I could give it feed and water every day."

Dad looked across the yard. "Out there is your wagon again," he said sadly. "You forgot to bring it in again, and now it is almost dark. You left some of your toys out in the yard, too."

Timmy hung his head. He knew Dad was right. He had a habit of leaving his wagon and other toys wherever he had played with them. Why hadn't he remembered to bring them in before supper? Slowly he went out to get them. "Maybe if I would always put my things away, Dad would let me have a rabbit," he thought.

In the days that followed, Timmy often thought of the rabbit he wanted. He tried hard to put his things away without being told. Soon it was no longer so hard to remember. Putting things away had become a habit.

Winter came. Timmy played out in the snow a lot. When it was too cold or too wet to play outside, he played in the house with his little sister Laura. He didn't think about asking for a rabbit now.

Spring came. Timmy helped Dad plow the garden. Then a nice warm day came and Mama wanted to plant the garden. She was in a hurry. "I want to plant potatoes, peas, lettuce, and onions before it rains again," she said. "Timmy, you will have to take care of Laura for me. You can play with her here in the yard and in the sandbox. But you must watch her all the time, so she doesn't get into trouble. If anything happens, you can call me. But you are responsible for Laura. It is up to you to see that she does not wander away and get lost."

Responsible! Timmy thought. *Dad said I have to learn to be responsible before I can have a rabbit. Maybe if I take good care of Laura, Dad and Mom will say I am old enough to take care of a rabbit.*

Laura was a little more than a year old. She was just starting to walk by herself, and she could say a few words. She really had to be watched every minute, because she could get into all kinds of things.

Mama put Laura into the sandbox and Timmy got in beside her. When Laura saw Mama hurrying away, she started to cry. "Here, Laura, you may have this bucket," Timmy said kindly. He gave Laura the nicest bucket and the biggest shovel. He showed her how to scoop up sand. Soon Laura stopped crying, and was a happy little girl.

When Laura stepped on Timmy's "farm" in the sandbox Timmy remembered not to hit her. When Laura got tired of the sandbox and crawled out, Timmy went along to see where she would go and what she would do. Soon Laura found a dandelion. She picked it and wanted to put it into her mouth.

"No, no!" Timmy laughed. "That's not good to eat."

Timmy ran to get his wagon, and pulled it back to Laura. Laura stood up, and Timmy lifted her into the wagon. "Ride! Ride!" Laura said.

Timmy pulled the wagon back and forth on the lane for awhile. Then Laura was thirsty. "Dwink!" she begged. "Dwink!" She pointed to the pump on the porch.

Timmy wanted to keep on playing, but he decided he had better give Laura a drink. He lifted her from the wagon, and held her hand as they walked to the porch.

Laura walked so slowly, but Timmy

let her take her time. He pumped water for Laura and then for himself.

By now Timmy was tired of watching Laura. He wished he could be out working with Dad. He wished Mama would come in from the garden and take Laura to the house with her. He went over to the swing and sat there, trying to make himself go. Just as the swing had picked up speed, Timmy saw Laura toddling down the hill toward the pasture fence. *I'm responsible for her,* Timmy remembered. He dragged his feet to stop the swing, and soon he was running after Laura again.

At last Mama came toward the house. She looked tired, but when she saw the children, she smiled. "Thank you, Timmy, for taking such good care of Laura!" she said. She took Laura to the house, changed her diaper, and put her in the highchair with a cracker. Then she quickly fixed dinner, while Timmy went out to put his wagon and their other toys away.

After dinner Mama put Laura to sleep. "I will go out to the garden again," she said. "You may rest here on the couch, and quietly look at these books. When Laura wakes up, call me quickly."

"Yes, Mom," said Timmy. He sat on the couch. He looked at every book in the stack Mama had given him. Then he lay down and fell asleep.

"WAAAH! WAH!" cried Laura.

Timmy sat up and rubbed his eyes. Where was Mama? Then he remembered. He got up from the couch and went to the door. "Mom!" he called as loudly as he could. "Laura's awake."

Mama came hurrying up from the garden. She got Laura, changed her diaper, and gave her a drink. "I would like to work in the garden for another hour," she said to Timmy. "Do you think you can watch Laura for me again?"

Timmy wished he could go along to the garden. That would be so much more fun than taking care of Laura. But he did not argue. He just said, "I will try."

Once more Mama put Laura into the

sandbox. Laura was cranky now, and cried for everything Timmy had. Finally Timmy gave up trying to make a farm, and just played with Laura. He was pouring sand on Laura's foot to make her laugh when suddenly he heard a loud noise.

"WOOF! WOOF!"

Timmy got up in a hurry and whirled around. There was the neighbor's big, mean dog, coming across the yard, right at them. That dog was not even supposed to be loose!

Timmy's heart thumped. He was afraid of that big dog. Once it had jumped up on him and knocked him down. He wanted to run into the house and shut

the door before that big dog got him. But he couldn't! He was responsible for Laura, and Laura could not run.

Timmy was so scared that his legs shook, but he stood right in front of his little sister. "Go away, you bad dog!" he shouted, waving the sand shovel at him.

The dog stopped, then came closer and barked again. Laura started to scream. Timmy almost jumped up and down in fright. "Go away!" he shouted. This time he threw his shovel at the dog.

Mama heard the noise and came running to see what was wrong. When the dog saw her, he ran away.

"Oh, Mom, I don't like that dog!" Timmy said. He was crying, too.

"That dog will go home and stay there, I think," Mama said. "I am finished planting now. I will take Laura into the house with me. You may do whatever you want until suppertime." She smiled at Timmy. "Thank you for being such a good helper."

At the supper table that evening, Mama told Dad how Timmy had watched Laura all day, and how he had tried to chase that big dog away.

"Well, well," Dad said, smiling. "I think Timmy is growing up."

"Daddy," said Timmy eagerly. "Do you think I am responsible enough to have a rabbit now?"

Dad looked at Mama and Mama looked at Dad. "Maybe you are," Dad said.

"We will see."

A few days later Dad went away. When he came back, he had not one, but *two* rabbits for Timmy! Timmy was very excited. The rabbits were so cute with their soft fur and long, floppy ears. Dad showed him how to feed them and give them clean water. "Remember, they are your rabbits," Dad said. "You are responsible for them."

Timmy smiled happily. He was going to try very hard to take care of his rabbits. He knew it should not be hard, now that he had learned to be responsible for other things.

Bread of deceit is sweet to a man; but afterwards his mouth shall be filled with gravel. Proverbs 20:17

Timmy and the Sugar

Timmy was four, and like all little boys and girls, he liked sweets. He liked ice cream, candy, cookies, and cakes with icing. He wished he could have those things to eat every day. But Timmy's Daddy and Mama were wise. They told him that if he ate too many sweets, he would not be strong and healthy.

Timmy even liked to taste sugar right out of the bag. "Mom, give me some sugar," he would beg when Mama was baking something. Sometimes she let him dip his finger into the sugar bag — just once.

"Mom, I like sugar so much, I could eat a whole bowl full," he said.

"Oh no," laughed Mama. "If you would try to eat so much sugar, you would not like it any more."

"Oh, yes, I would," Timmy said. He was sure he would always like sugar.

One morning Mama was working in the garden. Timmy helped for a while, but soon he got tired and went to play in the sandbox with his little sister Laura. Then he felt very hungry.

"Mom, may I have something to eat?" he called.

"Just wait, Timmy," came Mama's voice from the garden. "It will be time for lunch in half an hour. I want to finish picking these peas."

Timmy knew half an hour was a long time, especially when he was hungry. He played a minute longer, then stood up. He felt so hungry. He would go into the house and see if there was anything he could get for himself.

When Timmy entered the kitchen, the first thing he saw was a partly filled bag of sugar on the counter top, where Mama had been using it that morning. Timmy's tummy rumbled with hunger, and a naughty thought popped into his mind. This was his chance! Mama was out in the garden, and he was going to have as much sugar as he wanted — just this once.

Quietly Timmy pushed a chair over to the cupboard and reached up to get one of the plastic bowls Mama used to give him cereal for breakfast. He took a spoon and placed it in the bowl.

Next he carefully picked up the sugar

sack and tipped it over the bowl. The sack was heavy, but Timmy was strong. He let the sugar pour slowly into the bowl until it was half full. A pleased smile spread over Timmy's face. All that sugar, and he was going to eat every bite!

Timmy didn't forget to put the chair back at the table where it had been. Then he picked up his bowl of sugar and went quietly out the front door, carrying it in both hands. He went down the porch steps and crawled under the lilac bush. He knew Mom would not be pleased with what he was doing, so he wanted to hide to eat his sugar.

Timmy sat down. He took the bowl on his lap and ate a big bite of sugar.

"Hmmmm," he thought as he crunched the sugar with his teeth and the sweet taste spread through his mouth. Rapidly he gobbled a few more bites, and soon half the sugar was gone.

But now it seemed to Timmy that the sugar didn't taste as good as it had before. The spoon moved more slowly, and some of his teeth started to hurt. He tried to lick the sugar, rather than chewing it, but it made his mouth feel hot and bitter. Timmy decided he had had enough sugar, but there was still some left in the bowl.

Slowly Timmy ate several more little bites of sugar. Then he heard Mama and Laura coming in from the garden. Timmy's heart thumped. He took a huge bite of sugar, and nearly choked. He simply had to get rid of the rest of that sugar. He wished he had never taken all that sugar! It was very hard to eat the last bites, but finally he finished it.

Timmy stood up. His tummy hurt. Slowly he walked up the steps and into the house, leaving the bowl and the spoon under the bush. He felt a little dizzy.

"Oh, there you are, Timmy!" Mama said cheerfully. "Come, we are having strawberry shortcake for lunch." She set a bowl of bright red berries at his place, and began sprinkling sugar over them.

Sugar! Timmy's stomach felt as if a fish were flip-flopping inside it. His face turned pale, "Mom, I - I don't think I want any lunch," he stammered.

"Timmy!" Mama exclaimed. She sounded worried. "Are you sick, or have you done something you shouldn't have?"

Timmy began to cry. His mother was right. He *had* done something he wasn't supposed to, and he *was* sick, very sick! Of course, he had to tell Mama what he had done.

"I guess I won't need to spank you this time, Timmy," she said. "Being sick is your punishment for eating all that sugar."

Timmy just lay and groaned. His stomach hurt so much. He knew it would be a long time before he would even want to taste sugar again.

Let nothing be done through strife or vainglory.
Philippians 2:3.

Bossy Betty

"Let's play church now!" Betty said to her friends, Sharon and Kathy. Sharon's and Kathy's families had come to Betty's house for a Sunday evening visit, and the girls were eager to start playing.

"I'd rather play outside," said Sharon. "I never tried out your new swing yet."

"Oh, come on, Sharon!" Betty insisted. Betty was the oldest child in her family, and she was used to deciding what to play. "I want to play church first. We can swing after supper, before it gets dark."

Betty grabbed an armload of hymnbooks from the bookshelf.

"I'm going to bring our baby to hold," Kathy volunteered. "And do you have a purse I can use for a diaper bag?"

The three girls gathered several more of the smaller children, and went out to the front porch, where there was a long, high-backed wooden bench.

"Now, you sit here, Kathy," Betty ordered. "And Jennifer and baby Timmy will be your children."

"I want a baby to hold, too!" begged Sharon. "Can I hold Lucy?"

"No! Lucy is *my* little sister!" Betty argued. "But I guess you can have her when I get up to preach."

"Now, let's start singing." Betty told the children when they were all settled on the bench. "Jesus wants me for a Sunbeam!" she began lustily, and the others joined in.

The children sang "J-O-Y", and "Running Over", and "Jesus Loves Me". Then Kathy's brother Philip heard the singing and came out to the porch. "Can I play, too?" he asked.

"No! We don't want any boys!" Betty said rudely. "This game is only for girls and babies!"

"I could be the preacher," Philip told her. "You need a boy to preach."

"*I'm* going to be the preacher, 'cause I'm the biggest," said Betty, giving Philip a shove. "You go away."

"But Betty, girls aren't supposed to be preachers," Sharon reasoned. "The Bible says so."

"I don't care!" cried Betty. "This is my game, and I don't want him in it! Sit still, Lucy," she added squeezing her little sister tighter as she tried to climb down from Betty's lap.

But the other girls had had enough. "You're just too bossy, Betty," Sharon declared.

"Bossy Betty!" Kathy giggled. "That sounds right."

"Bossy Betty!" "Bossy Betty!" Philip and Jennifer chimed in.

Betty's face burned, and tears came

to her eyes. Choking back sobs, she turned and ran. Where could she hide? There! Nobody was in her bedroom. Betty slammed the door shut and flopped down on her bed, crying hot tears of anger and shame.

Suddenly Mother was sitting on the bed beside her. "Betty, what is wrong?" she asked quietly.

"They - they called me 'Bossy Betty'!" the little girl wept. "They don't want to play like I say!"

"Betty, sit up," her mother said firmly. "I know it makes you feel upset if the other children call you names. But it sounds like you *were* being bossy. When you have guests, you must play what they want to play. And you should have let Philip be the preacher. Now blow your nose, and come into the kitchen."

Mother stood up and looked out the window. "The other girls are playing happily on the swing now," she told Betty. "Come and help me put the food on the table, and after supper you can try again to play nicely with your friends."

Meekly, Betty followed her mother to the kitchen. *After supper I will let the other girls choose what to play,* she decided to herself. *I don't want to be 'Bossy Betty' anymore!*

Thou shalt honor the face of the old . . .
Leviticus 19:32.

Going for a Visit

"We are going to visit Sister Mary Weaver today," Dad said one afternoon when Sharon and Peter were in school. Then he added, "Old people sometimes don't like noise, so I want you children to be quiet and respectful."

"What is 'respectful'?" asked Timmy.

"When you are quiet and polite, that is being respectful," Dad explained.

"Will there be toys for us to play with?" asked Laura.

"She may not have many," Mama said.

"Sister Mary lives in a little house, and no children live with her. We will take one doll along for Laura, and a toy car for Timmy. Then we want you to sit quietly and play with them."

Soon the family was on their way. "Is this lady very old?" Timmy asked.

"Yes," replied Dad. "She is probably the oldest person you have ever seen. When people get very old, sometimes their bodies don't work so well anymore. That is why Sister Mary is in a wheelchair. Her legs are not strong enough for her to walk anymore."

Laura thought about how easy it was for her to run. What if her legs would be too old and weak to walk?

"Old people have lived a long time, and have learned a lot," Dad went on. "That is why we must be respectful to them and listen to what they have to say."

Soon they were at Mrs. Weaver's house. Dad knocked on the door.

"Come in!" the old lady called cheerfully.

Timmy and Laura stepped quietly into the room and smiled at Sister Mary, sitting there in her wheelchair. They shook hands politely, then sat down to listen to the grownups' talk.

Laura rocked her doll for a while, then carried her quietly around the room to show her the flowers. Suddenly she saw a very big and pretty flower. "Mom! What

kind of flower is this?" she asked. "It has three big, bright flowers."

Mama did not answer right away. She put her hand on Laura's arm and went right on talking to Sister Mary.

Laura hung her head, feeling ashamed. She had been so excited, she had not noticed that Mama was talking.

At last Mama turned to her and said, "What did you want, Laura?"

"What kind of flower is that?" she asked, pointing. "It is very pretty."

"That is a gloxinia," Mary answered with a smile. "I am glad you like it."

Just then Timmy's toy car went Zoom! Zoom! Zoom! across the floor. He forgot about being quiet and respectful.

"Shhh! Timmy, not so loud," Dad said.

Timmy made his car go more quietly. It was more fun to zoom loudly, but he wanted to be respectful.

After what seemed like a long time to Laura and Timmy, Dad said it was time to go home.

"Wait a minute," said Sister Mary. "The children were so nice and quiet, I want to give them something." She wheeled her chair out to the kitchen, and was soon back with a little bag. She gave it to Laura.

"Thank you!" Laura said. She peeped into the bag, and let Timmy look, too. "Six big cookies!" she said out loud. "We can each have one for supper, and Sharon and Peter, too."

Mary Weaver smiled. "Yes, that is what they are for," she said.

When they were all in the car and on the way home, Dad said, "Thank you, children, for being so nice and quiet. Sister Mary appreciated it, and we did, too."

"I forgot once and interrupted Mom when she was talking," Laura said, hanging her head. "I'm sorry."

"I forgot, too, and made my car go loudly," Timmy said. "I'm sorry."

"You tried hard, didn't you?" Mama replied. "We are glad you are learning to be respectful."

Laura felt good inside. Being respectful made her happy.

A righteous man regardeth the life of his beast, but the . . . wicked are cruel. Proverbs 12:10.

Timmy's Goat

Toot, toot! Sounded the horn as the Miller's black station wagon pulled into the lane.

"Daddy's home!" Timmy shouted, running across the yard. "But, oh!" his eyes grew round with surprise. "*What* is that in the back of the car?"

A funny little face was peering out the window. Long floppy ears, bright yellow-brown eyes, tiny stubs of horns on top — and then a second little face popped up beside the first! "Goats! Two baby goats in the car?" Timmy gasped, hardly able to believe his eyes.

Daddy Miller opened his car door and stepped out. "Surprise!" he told Timmy with a big grin. "Uncle Leonard gave us these two kids, since I have been doing his chores for him while his broken leg heals. We put them into feed sacks for the trip home." He opened the rear door of the station wagon as he spoke. Each little goat was in a feed sack, with a draw-string tied around his neck! They looked so funny.

"Ba-a-ah!" they cried as Daddy lifted them out one by one. Gently he took off the feed sacks and set them free on the grass.

Timmy's big brother Peter heard the

noise, and came out of the house. "Kids!"
he cried excitedly. "Are they for us?"

"Yes, boys. These kids will be yours,
if you take good care of them," Daddy
said. "There is one for each of you."

"I want this one!" Timmy declared.
"With the brown spots. I will call him
Buster."

"You boys will need to give your goats
a bottle of milk every morning and

evening, because they are still very young," Daddy told them. He took two black rubber objects from his pocket. "Here are some special nipples that are just the right size for kids; we will put them onto pop bottles, and that's what you can use to feed milk to your pets."

Peter and Timmy took good care of their little goats. They fed them lots of milk, hay, and grain-pellets. Soon Buster and Blackie, Peter's goat, grew big and strong. The boys had a lot of fun playing with their pet goats!

One day Timmy had an idea. "I wonder if I could ride on my goat's back?" he said to Peter. "Buster is so big now, I'm sure he could carry me!"

"You'd better ask Daddy first," Peter told him.

"Yes, I believe you could ride on your goat, if he will let you," Daddy said, looking at the slender six-year-old. "Peter mustn't try it, though. He would be too heavy."

"Yay!" Timmy cheered happily. Quick as a flash, he was back outdoors and running to the pasture where the goats were grazing.

"Buster! Buster! Ba-a-ah!" called Timmy, and there was an answering "Ba-a-ah!" as the goat trotted to meet him. Buster looked eagerly at his young master as if to say, "What did you bring for me to eat?"

"It's not feeding time yet, Buster," said Timmy, stroking his pet's neck. "I'm going to teach you a new trick, instead." Carefully he took hold of the goat's horns, and climbed onto his back. "Now, Buster, Giddyap!" he ordered.

Buster turned his head to stare in surprise at Timmy. "Ba-a-ah!" he grunted, and tried to shake off the strange weight on his back. "No, Buster!" cried Timmy. "Giddyap and go!" But Buster would not go forward.

Timmy tried again and again, but his goat would not do what he wanted. Buster kept trying to shake him off. He dug his hooves stubbornly into the ground and refused to move. Sometimes he would take a few steps backward, but he never moved in the right direction!

Timmy was getting hot and frustrated. "I know what I need," he decided at last. "I need a *whip* to make this goat go!" He ran over to the fence row and chose a tall, tough-looking weed. "This will teach Buster to go," Timmy muttered as he began to pull. But the big weed was as stubborn as the goat! Timmy set his feet wide apart and pulled with all his might. Suddenly the big weed came bursting up out of the ground, and Timmy sat down with a hard thump. "Owww!" he cried as he stood up, rubbing his sore bottom.

"*Now* that goat had better go," Timmy

growled as he stalked across the field, stripping the leaves from his switch.

"Giddyap, Buster!" he commanded sternly as soon as he was seated on the goat's back once more. But again the bewildered Buster would not move forward, so Timmy raised his switch and brought it down smartly across the goat's rump. "Ba-a-ah!" cried Buster. Down went his head, up came his back. Before Timmy knew what was happening, he had hit the ground again . . . landing on his head this time!

"You mean goat!" Timmy cried as he got to his feet. "I'll teach you not to buck me off!" Gripping the switch, he started after Buster, who was dancing around nervously just out of reach.

"Wait, Timmy!" Daddy's deep voice stopped him. "What is going on?" Timmy turned to see his father standing at the fence.

"Oh, Daddy!" wailed Timmy. "Buster just won't *go* when I sit on his back! And when I whipped him, he bucked me off!"

"Whipping your goat won't work, I'm afraid," Daddy told Timmy. "Buster will just get scared of you if you treat him like that. He will soon learn to think, 'Here comes the boy that hurts me,' and will run away when he sees you."

"How can I train him, then?" Timmy asked, sadly.

"Well," his father encouraged, "I'm

sure you can figure out something. You will need to think of a way to make Buster *want* to go forward. How about using something he likes to eat?"

Timmy sat down in the warm, sunny pasture to think. Suddenly his eyes brightened. Jumping up, he ran to the big old maple tree that stood beside the pasture fence. Several branches hung low enough to reach, and sometimes Daddy would break off a small bunch of leaves as a treat for the goats. Now Timmy picked a leafy branch about three feet long, and went to look for Buster once more.

"Ba-a-ah! Come, Buster!" he called. This time the goat came more cautiously.

But when he saw what Timmy had, he trotted faster! Timmy let Buster nibble a few of the leaves, while he climbed onto the goat's back. Then he held the branch just out of reach in front of Buster's face. "Giddyap, Buster!" he ordered excitedly. And now, eager for more of the delicious maple leaves, Buster moved forward at last!

"So, I finally got a good ride," Timmy reported to the rest of the Millers at supper, "by using kindness instead of a whip! Now Buster and I can have even more fun together."

In like manner also, that women adorn them-selves in modest apparel. I Timothy 2:9.

It's Safer To Be Plain

Slowly the screen door swung shut behind Laura, and slowly she made her way into the warm kitchen. Mama was just taking a panful of hot golden-brown cookies from the oven, but today Laura hardly noticed the delicious smell.

"Hello, Laura!" her mother cheerfully greeted the first grader as she dropped her new lunch box on the counter. "What's wrong with my sunshiny girl today? Are you tired of school, after only three days?"

"No," the six-year-old replied unhappily.

"I like the teacher, and I like math and learning to read. But . . ." her voice trailed off.

"But what, Laura?" Mama encouraged her.

"Well, the other girls said my dress isn't pretty," Laura grumbled. "It's too plain!" She looked down at the new blue school dress which had made her so happy when Mama first finished it.

"I said, 'My dress is, too, pretty!' But Becky and Sarah laughed and said it was just an Amish dress. Sarah said, 'Look, I have ruffles on my skirt and a bow on top. Your dress doesn't have anything!' And Jennifer's dress had pretty little dots all through the cloth; and Becky's Mom makes fancy stitches all around her neck and sleeves . . . she said it was called 'abroidery'."

Laura looked sadly at her mother. "Why do we have to wear clothes that are plain?" she asked.

Mama sat down and lifted her daughter onto her lap. Smiling down into the troubled little face, she said softly, "Laura, sometimes it *is* hard to be different. But that's the way life is: we need to do what we believe is right, even though others don't. Wearing plain, simple clothing makes it easier for us to serve the Lord, because we don't need to waste a lot of time and money on fancy things. And anyway, it's safer to be plain."

"What do you mean, Mama?" Laura asked, snuggling closer to her mother.

"Well, that reminds me of a story that was written by a wise man named Aesop, many hundreds of years ago."

"Tell it!" begged Laura.

"Well," Mama began, "Once a large, orange and black butterfly came to rest on the branch of a tree. As it sat lazily fanning those bright wings in the sunshine, suddenly it noticed a moth already on the branch! The gray moth clung to the branch with wings folded down, looking just like the bark on the tree.

"'How plain you are,' the butterfly said mockingly, fluttering her own golden wings. 'You have no color at all! I almost didn't see you were here. Don't you wish you were beautiful, like me?' But just as she spoke, a small hawk spied the bright wings. Swooping down from the sky, he seized her in his sharp talons . . . and that was the end of the beautiful, boastful butterfly.

"But the plain, gray little moth sat

safely on her branch. The hawk hadn't noticed her."

Laura giggled. "I guess it really is safer to be plain," she admitted, sliding down from her mother's lap. "I'll go change out of my new dress now, so I won't get it dirty . . . and then may I have some cookies, Mama?"

Thy Word is a lamp unto my feet, and a light unto my path. Psalm 119:105

Benny's Bible

His very own new Bible! Benny was so thrilled as he stood gazing at the book which his father had just placed in his hands.

It was a real, grown-up Bible, but small and supple in Benny's hands. Lifting it to his face, Benny sniffed the fragrance of the new leather. "Thank you, Daddy!" he breathed happily. I'll try to take good care of it!"

And Benny did. He took his new Bible along to church the next Sunday, and turned the crisp, thin pages so gently to find each reference. After church was dismissed, he carried his Bible out to the car and put it safely inside before going to talk with his friends. At home Benny's little sister wanted to hold his new Bible. Benny wanted to be kind, so he let her; but only for a moment, while he watched anxiously.

One Sunday evening a few weeks later, Benny walked out of the church door with his best friend Peter Miller. As the boys stood talking, Benny noticed that his shoe was untied. Carefully he set his Bible on the trunk of the Millers' car nearby, and bent to fasten his shoelace. Just as he was finished, a girl screamed -

- "Eeeek! Look at that big bug!"

Benny jerked upright and ran to look, with Peter and the other boys, completely forgetting his Bible.

Not until he was in the car, on the way home with his family, did Benny think of the Bible. "Where is my . . . does anyone have my Bible?" he exclaimed, feeling around on the seat. Daddy switched on the dome light, and the family searched the car. But the Bible was nowhere to be found!

"You must have left it at church," Mother said. "Shall we go back and look?"

Daddy turned the car around and headed back into the churchyard, but Benny could not find his Bible there. He hunted through the benches in the sanctuary, but found no Bible. He looked into the restroom, although he hadn't been there all evening. On the cloakroom shelf there were no Bibles, either, except for a very old one belonging to someone else.

"It's time to go home," Daddy said. "Maybe you forgot to bring your Bible along tonight?" Benny shook his head. He was sure he had had his Bible. "Well, we will pray about it," said Mother. "The Lord knows where your Bible is, and it will surely turn up."

Meanwhile, the Millers' car was also leaving the churchyard and heading for home, down a different road. In the darkness, nobody noticed the small black Bible lying on the trunk of the black car. Nobody but God! God saw that the Bible did not fall as the car turned a corner. He watched as the Millers' car picked up speed to climb a hill. Just at the right moment, God allowed the Bible to slide from its perch and land in the soft grass beside the road.

Benny was sad that night as he lay in his bed and looked at the empty shelf where his Bible should have been. "Please, God, help me to find my Bible!" he prayed before he fell asleep.

Next morning, while Benny was in school, the telephone rang. "Hello," his mother answered politely.

"Do you have anyone in your family named Benny?" the caller asked. "And did he lose a Bible?"

The caller was a neighbor lady who lived about a mile away. She told Benny's mother that when she had walked out to her mailbox that morning she had seen a Bible lying in the grass. "It was right under my mailbox!" the lady said. "I couldn't imagine how it got there, but I knew somebody would be missing that nice Bible!"

Benny's mother thanked the lady, and told her that they would come over to get the Bible.

How much happier Benny felt that evening, with his precious Bible in his hands once more! He sniffed the rich new leather of the cover, and carefully turned the fragile pages. Yes, the Bible was safe. Benny found his favorite verse, in Psalm 119: "Thy Word is a lamp unto my feet, and a light unto my path."

I'll be more careful next time, Benny promised himself. And he prayed, "Thank you, Lord, for giving me back my Bible."

Thou shalt not steal.   Exodus 20:15

Mama and the Silver Dollar

"Mama, tell us a story," Laura begged, as she and Timmy helped their mother snap green beans one hot summer afternoon.

"Yes, Mama, a story about *you* when you were a little girl!" Timmy chimed in.

"All right," Mama agreed cheerfuly. "Shall I tell a summer story or a winter story?"

"A winter story, please," Timmy answered with a sigh. "It's *so* hot today."

"Well, on a winter night many years ago," Mama began, "my parents decided to go visit a neighbor. Mrs. Yoder was a widow who lived alone, not far from our house. So we all put on our coats, and mittens and boots, and went outside into the frosty cold. My mother carried the baby in his snowsuit, and my father carried little Aunt Rosa. I was three or four years old, so I could walk by myself, and I can still remember how the snow crunched under my little boots."

Snow! Timmy thought, shivering deliciously. Suddenly he didn't feel hot any more, just comfortable and warm.

"Mrs. Yoder was old, and had no children living with her," Mama went on. "So I didn't have much to do after we came to her house. While the grownups talked, I moved silently around the room looking at Mrs. Yoder's plants, pictures and knick-nacks. There was a bedroom beside the living room, and I slipped through the open door. Nobody called me back, so I looked around this room too. The only thing I saw to interest a little girl was a tray of different small objects on the nightstand.

"There was a keychain, and a few pill bottles, a little carved wooden elephant and some pins and coins. I looked long-ingly at the money. There were pennies, nickles, dimes and quarters, and even a big silver dollar!"

"What's a silver dollar?" Laura wondered.

"When I was a little girl, people used

one-dollar coins as well as dollar bills," Mama explained.

"I was too young to know what the different coins were, but I liked that big shiny silver dollar. Slowly I reached out my hand and touched it . . . then picked it up. The coin was cool and heavy in my little hand. *I'd like to put this big money in my piggy bank!* I thought covetously. And do you know what I did then?" Mama paused, looking sadly at the children.

"Did you steal it, Mom?" Timmy frowned, and Laura's eyes were big.

"Yes, that's what I did," Mama said softly. "I took that silver dollar and put it into my dress pocket. Then I hurried out of the bedroom and climbed onto the couch to sit between my parents. I was very quiet for the rest of the visit. All the while, as I sat on the couch, I could feel that big coin pressing against my leg. *When I get home, I'll put the big money in my piggy bank!* I thought, but I felt guilty too. *That isn't yours, Mrs. Yoder didn't give it to you!* my conscience told me. *Mommy and Daddy wouldn't like it if they found out!*

Findly the visit was over. We put on our coats and boots again, and said goodbye to Mrs. Yoder. Stars were twinkling in the frosty sky as we crunched home through the snow. But I didn't enjoy this walk so much as the first one! The silver dollar was in my coat pocket now, and I was not happy. What would happen if my parents saw it? I lagged behind, with one hand in my pocket clutching the silver dollar. Soon we were home, and taking off our coats. I tried to slip the silver dollar into my dress pocket, but I wasn't quick enough. 'What do you have in your hand?' my mother asked in surprise. 'Where did you get that silver dollar?' Daddy wanted to know. I was caught!

'"You must not take other people's things,' my parents told me sternly when they found out where I had picked up the money. 'That was stealing, and God does not want us to steal! Taking somebody else's money is very naughty.'

"Tears began to run down my cheeks, and my parents looked at each other. 'I will take her back to Mrs. Yoder's right now, while you put the others to bed,' Daddy said. 'She can give back the money and tell Mrs. Yoder that she is sorry. That will be the right thing to do.'

"So my coat and boots were put on again, for the third time that evening. For the third time, I walked out into the snowy night. Soon we were at Mrs. Yoder's again, and my daddy handed me the silver dollar. 'You may give this back to the lady yourself, and tell her that you are sorry,' he said. 'I will help you to explain what you did.' Then he knocked on the door."

Laura shivered, thinking of that little girl long ago, and how ashamed she must have been when she returned the stolen money.

"I'm sure you never wanted to steal anything more, ever again!" she said solemnly.

"You're right," Mama smiled. "The Bible tells us that 'Thou shalt not steal,' and my parents showed me how important it is to obey this commandment. It has been thirty years since that snowy night, but I have never forgotten the lesson of the silver dollar."

Also by Mildred A. Martin:

Missionary Stories with the Millers
Thrilling adventures of real Christian missionaries
All ages

Prudence and the Millers
Stories and Scripture lessons on courtesy,
health and safety. Ages 7-14

Prudence and Your Health
Workbook for Prudence and the Millers
Fourth to sixth grade level

School Days with the Millers
The Miller children live and learn valuable lessons —
at school and at home. Ages 7-14

Wisdom and the Millers
(Proverbs for Children)
25 chapters illustrating great truths of life in
story form. Ages 6-13

Working with Wisdom
Workbook for Wisdom and the Millers
Third and fourth grade level

Make and Do with the Millers
Creativity and coloring for preschoolers

Inquire at your favorite book dealer or write to:
ı E mail: greenpastures@emypeople.net

Green Pastures Press
HC 67, Box 91-A
Mifflin, PA 17058